IMAGES
of America

SPRINGFIELD ARMORY

Pictured here around 1880 are the Hill Shops of Springfield Armory. This is the oldest section of the armory, the land first used as an ordnance storage depot, or arsenal, and workshops during the American Revolution. Seen from the intersection of State and Federal Streets, this block forms the core of Springfield Armory National Historic Site, which was established by Congress in 1974 to commemorate the national importance of Springfield Armory. (Courtesy of Springfield Armory National Historic Site.)

On the Cover: Taken on September 30, 1886, this image shows the employees of the stocking shop at Springfield Armory. Each person, dressed in their work clothes, holds the implements of their respective jobs as they each labored to craft black walnut stocks for the Springfield "Trapdoor" Rifle. (Courtesy of Springfield Armory National Historic Site.)

IMAGES
of America

SPRINGFIELD ARMORY

Alex MacKenzie

ARCADIA
PUBLISHING

ISBN 978-1-4671-2274-0

Published by Arcadia Publishing
Charleston, South Carolina

Printed in the United States of America

Library of Congress Control Number: 2014942882

For all general information, please contact Arcadia Publishing:
Telephone 843-853-2070
Fax 843-853-0044
E-mail sales@arcadiapublishing.com
For customer service and orders:
Toll-Free 1-888-313-2665

Visit us on the Internet at www.arcadiapublishing.com

To all the volunteers at Springfield Armory National Historic Site, who tirelessly help preserve the history of Springfield Armory

Contents

Acknowledgments

I would first and foremost like to thank the staff and management of Springfield Armory National Historic Site for their support in creating this book, which was a long time coming. I do not say it as often as I should, but thank you guys, so much. Unless otherwise noted, all images appearing in this book came from the archival collections at Springfield Armory National Historic Site.

The museum at Springfield Armory has been around for a long, long time—since the years immediately following the Civil War. Curators and museum staff have come and gone over those years, but the volunteers that come to the museum each day have been critical to its success. I would like to thank the volunteers, interns, students, and other hangers-on, without whom none of this would be possible.

Another round of thanks goes to the Springfield Armory Alliance, the support organization for Springfield Armory National Historic Site, for all they do to help preserve museum and archival collections, grounds, and buildings for the benefit of future generations of park visitors. Keep 'em coming!

Thanks also to Caitrin Cunningham at Arcadia Publishing, whose technical feedback and patience have made this effort go as smoothly as possible. Additionally, profuse thanks are due to Maggie Humberston and Cliff McCarthy at the Lyman and Merrie Wood Museum of Springfield History and Michelle Hammer at Harpers Ferry National Historical Park who helped me find several important images for the book.

Finally, I would like to thank my family for their unwavering support and belief in me.

INTRODUCTION

When Secretary of Defense Robert McNamara announced the impending closure of Springfield Armory on November 19, 1964, the community of Springfield, Massachusetts, was shocked. Reams of reports were coming from Department of Defense analysts justifying the closure and citing a range of issues but mostly arguing for cost-effectiveness. Why spend government funds on the employment and machinery to produce small arms for the military when a final product could simply be purchased by contract? But the statistics, graphs, models, and cold words announcing Springfield Armory was "excess to the needs of the federal government" did not make sense to those who worked there, nor did it make sense to those who saw the benefits Springfield Armory had on the region. However, if they had asked anyone who was involved with the creation of the government armories 170 years before, they might not have been so surprised.

The story of how Springfield Armory arrived at this point goes back to the very founding of the United States of America. With France entering the American Revolution in support of the rebellious colonies, the Continental Army received the supplies it desperately needed to fight in pitched battles with the British. Muskets, pistols, cannon, ammunition, and other materiel arrived en masse. The supplies arriving in New England were immediately sent to storage depots, or arsenals, like the one established at Springfield in 1777. From there, the supplies were distributed to the soldiers fighting in New York and other areas.

After the war, the arsenal at Springfield remained stocked with French muskets and other supplies, but many in the American government recognized the need to be militarily self-sustaining like other nations. With congressional authorization, and endorsement by President Washington in 1794, the new armories, or arms factories, at Springfield, Massachusetts, and Harpers Ferry, Virginia, had a daunting task in front of them. Essentially, the government needed to start up two musket factories in two different parts of the country at a time when industry as we now know it did not yet exist. Where Springfield was able to get a quick start making muskets in 1795 because of the existing arsenal buildings and workforce, Harpers Ferry, with no infrastructure at all, would not begin producing until the early 1800s.

In order to support government production at the armories, the War Department embarked on a plan to develop a more robust private small arms industry in the United States. In 1798, a contract was advertised to manufacture muskets for $13.40 apiece and awarded to inventor Eli Whitney in New Haven, Connecticut. A year later, a contract for pistol manufacture was given to Simeon North of Middletown, Connecticut. Thus began the government subsidy of the fledgling firearm industry in the United States. But, like Springfield and Harpers Ferry Armories, many of these new factories began effectively from and with nothing. Arms factories are quite specialized, and even though many outfits created other items (contractors Simeon North and Nathan Starr of Middletown both made farm implements), plenty of new capital is needed to procure and install the required tooling, purchase materials, and hire labor. According to one estimate at the time, it took two years to establish an arms factory and an additional 20 years for that investment to make a profit.

The War Department recognized these challenges and structured contracts to enable these new factories to get off the ground. Usually, contracts were written for five years, and they often came with significant advances. Eli Whitney received so many advances, that when his 1798 contract was complete, he was owed less than two percent of the total contracted amount. In addition, the $13.40 per musket contract price was well above the $10 or so it cost the government to manufacture the same weapon at Springfield Armory. This discrepancy was intentional.

With this favorable contract system came an interchange of ideas, equipment, and expertise that further solidified private industry. Wage competition moved experienced employees between government armories and other companies in the 1820s and 1830s; this included new textile factories and other industries springing up around the country. Thomas Blanchard, who famously invented the irregular lathe and installed the machines at Springfield and Harpers Ferry Armories, also installed similar machinery in the private sector. Inspectors from the armories would recognize talented workers and persuade them to come work at Springfield, and contractors visiting Springfield Armory would lure talent away to private factories.

In the 1840s, the government declared that it no longer needed to provide overly favorable terms and could award contracts to the company that provided the bid most appealing to the government. New firms were established over the following years that were fully capable of standing on their own products in addition to securing government contracts, including Ames Manufacturing in Chicopee, Massachusetts; Robbins and Lawrence in Windsor, Vermont; Colt in Hartford, Connecticut; Smith and Wesson in Springfield, Massachusetts; Christian Sharps in Hartford, Connecticut; and Christopher Spencer in Boston, among many others.

In a hint of things to come, by 1853, Congressional representatives voiced their concerns about the management of the armories and pushed for the sole use of contractors by government procurement agents. It was a persuasive argument, but the armories were saved by none other than the then current secretary of war, Jefferson Davis. The report, issued on December 1, 1853 read, in part, "It follows that it would not be advisable to make all arms by contract. Neither would I think it wise to restrict the manufacture of all arms to the national armories . . . it is still more important that the government should have the power to contract for the manufacture of arms in the event of an exigency under which a greater number might be required than the public armories, upon a scale adapted to ordinary circumstances, would be able to supply."

The government armories were saved, but the Civil War demonstrated a serious issue with the armory system that had been lingering for almost 70 years. Legally, Springfield Armory could not get additional funding until Congress declared war, which left the officers in charge scrambling to dramatically increase employment, machinery, tooling, and thus production in the earliest days of the conflict. This was the case in World War I as well. Contracts were heavily relied upon to supplement production and ensure that the military would have the weapons it needed. While Springfield Armory was much more prepared for World War II, a postwar shift in policy dictated that production would rely heavily on contracts and the primary role of the armory would shift to research and development.

This signified the beginning of the end of Springfield Armory. McNamara's accountant, echoing many of the arguments made a century earlier, determined that private, small arms contractors could meet the production needs of the military, and the research and development functions could move to other facilities. Ironically, once the small arms industry that Springfield Armory helped nurture became fully capable and self-sustaining, it rendered the armory obsolete.

Still, by the time Springfield Armory was closed on April 30, 1968, it left quite a legacy behind. The Continental Arsenal established by George Washington provided supplies that helped win the American Revolution. After the armory began manufacturing, again, with Washington's approval, weapons that were crafted by armory workers (and several that were invented and developed in-house) were in the hands of the US military in all major American conflicts since the War of 1812. The armory also helped to establish private industry, exchanging ideas, workers, and machinery that helped to realize the goal of manufacturing interchangeable parts, launching the American Industrial Revolution. Springfield Armory, for all it accomplished over nearly two centuries, will always be inextricably linked with the history of Springfield, Massachusetts; the history of New England; the history of the United States; and beyond.

One

1777–1814

In January 1776, scores of oxen pulling sleds laden with heavy artillery stopped in Springfield, Massachusetts, for some rest. Col. Henry Knox, leading the long line of artillery transported from Fort Ticonderoga, was on his way to Boston, or at least the outskirts, to set up the cannon and fire on the town. The Redcoats were there, and General Washington wanted them gone.

Knox left Springfield with his refreshed teams heading east along the old Boston Road. As he crested the rise overlooking the town, he doubtless looked out onto the open plain. Sparsely populated, the plain was sandy due to its past as a prehistoric lake bottom and unsuited for agriculture. Knox would argue for the government use of this land, which he deemed a perfect place for an arsenal that would store military supplies and house a laboratory as a workshop for repairs and minor fabrication. Less than a year later, the Continental Arsenal at Springfield was established.

Knox again argued for Springfield when the time came to begin government manufacture of shoulder arms to support the new nation's military. He liked that the town was positioned along major land routes—the same that he used to bring his artillery to Boston and the same that would be needed to distribute military supplies to arsenals around the country. The town also sat on the Connecticut River, north of a series of shallows near Windsor, Connecticut, that made the river unnavigable for large warships. The plain's elevated position above the town and river also provided a defensible position should invaders make it that far. Also, the area had a good supply of skilled labor and water access to power machinery. In 1794, the arsenal became an armory, or arms factory, and began manufacturing within a year.

George Washington, as commanding general of the Continental Army, was instrumental in the establishment of arsenals and other storage depots that would supply his army. Logistics would prove instrumental in supplying the Continental Army during the American Revolution. (Courtesy of the Library of Congress.)

Gen. Henry Knox, as Washington's chief of artillery, was primarily responsible for the selection of potential arsenal sites. Among the locations considered were Carlisle, Pennsylvania; Hartford, Connecticut; and Brookfield, Massachusetts. Ultimately, Knox recommended Springfield, Massachusetts, as the ideal location. (Courtesy of the Library of Congress.)

A variety of military supplies arrived at Springfield from all over the world. This included muskets, such as the French Charleville. Here, Marshal Ferdinand Foch, Supreme Allied Commander during World War I, holds one of these early muskets while visiting Springfield Armory in 1921. To his left is Lt. Col. Julian Hatcher. Arms and supplies from the French, who supported American independence, arrived on the New England coast and were transported to Springfield for storage until they were distributed in the field.

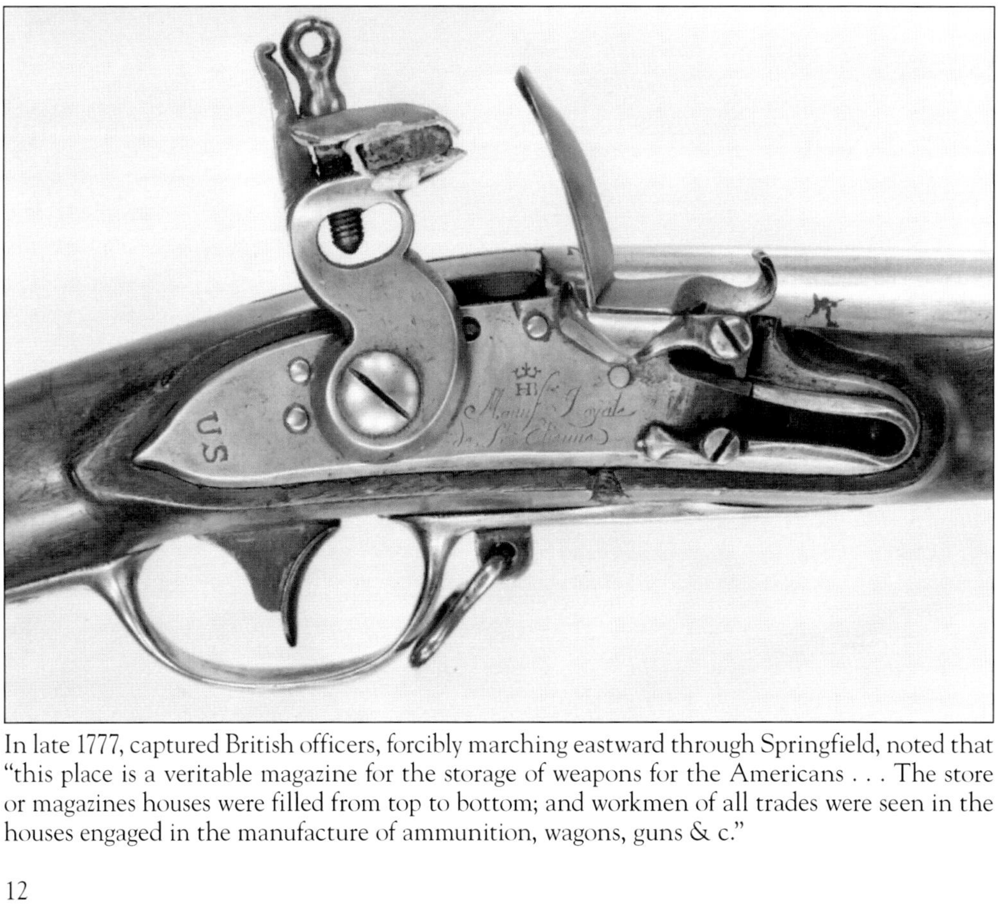

In late 1777, captured British officers, forcibly marching eastward through Springfield, noted that "this place is a veritable magazine for the storage of weapons for the Americans . . . The store or magazines houses were filled from top to bottom; and workmen of all trades were seen in the houses engaged in the manufacture of ammunition, wagons, guns & c."

Lt. Col. David Mason, the first officer in charge of the laboratory at Springfield, had the title of director of ordnance. Hundreds of men reported to Lieutenant Colonel Mason, who paid his workmen with funds appropriated from the Continental Treasury. Some of the workmen were enlisted for three years in a detachment of artillery artificers, which included carpenters, metal smiths, wheelwrights, and harness makers, among others. Civilian laborers were hired for rote work. The main role of the laboratory was the "repair and replacement of arms and artillery equipment, and . . . the fabrication of cartridges and fuses." Over one week alone, arsenal workers produced over 7,500 cartridges.

With the end of the American Revolution in 1781, the laboratory function of the arsenal was over, but it continued to serve as storage. In addition to the storage of muskets and other military supplies, this brick magazine was constructed in 1782 as a safe place to store mass quantities of explosive black powder. The building was demolished in the 1840s, and later, Magazine Street was laid over the site and named for the old structure.

Among the soldiers stationed at the arsenal during the American Revolution was John Bryant, who began his career as an officer in an artillery regiment. He was promoted to captain and placed in charge of the arsenal in 1781. Bryant continued to serve there as paymaster and military storekeeper after the Springfield Armory was established.

A growing rebellion in western Massachusetts came to a climax at Springfield Arsenal in January 1787. A group known as the Regulators, led by Daniel Shays, finding no relief from Massachusetts's unfair system of tax collection, resolved to address their grievances with open-armed revolt. Thousands of rebels, aiming to secure military weaponry and supplies, briefly battled a hired militia at Springfield Arsenal. The Regulators were not successful, though their efforts affected the debates at the Constitutional Convention a few months later. Pictured here is the Wait Monument, a Masonic marker placed along what is now State Street in 1763. It is the last surviving structure that existed at the time of Shays' Rebellion.

George Washington visited Springfield on October 24, 1789, and stayed at the Parsons Tavern in town, pictured above. While inspecting the arsenal buildings, which were public property, he noted, "Reached Springfield by 4 o'clock, and while dinner was getting examined the Continental stores at this place, which I found in very good order at the buildings (on the hill above the town), which belong to the United States. The barracks (also public property) are going fast to destruction, and in a little time will be no more, without repair. The laboratory, which seems to be a good building, is in tolerably good repair, and the powder magazine, which is of brick, seems to be in excellent order and the powder in it very dry." (Courtesy of the Lyman and Merrie Wood Museum of Springfield History.)

With relationships with other major world powers on a decline, the United States recognized the need to manufacture military weaponry within its borders. In 1794, Congress passed an act authorizing President Washington to establish magazines, arsenals, and armories. As some facilities existed and there was ample waterpower, the arsenal at Springfield became an armory. Washington also selected Harpers Ferry, Virginia (above, about 1840), as the site of a second armory. Together, these government armories would produce firearms for the Army and militia throughout the United States. (Courtesy of Harpers Ferry National Historical Park.)

The new armories were each organized under a civilian superintendent who was appointed by the president. David Ames, a local businessman, was appointed as Springfield Armory's first superintendent and would oversee operations until 1802. The first musket produced at Springfield Armory was based on the French Charleville musket. This gun was the standard Army infantry weapon when the United States went to war with Britain again during the War of 1812. Between 1795 and 1814, about 85,000 of these models were made.

Shortly after it received authorization to begin manufacturing, the government sought to secure more land for this purpose. The site of the arsenals and other buildings had no source of power. A mile south of this area, land was purchased on the Mill River, seen here, which could be dammed to harness waterpower. Materials for manufacture flowed into the armory from various locales. Much of the steel used came from England; grindstones came from Nova Scotia; coal came from Virginia and Pennsylvania; bar and rolled iron came from Connecticut and Pennsylvania; and black walnut came from Pennsylvania, New York, and later Ohio.

The major goal of the federal armories was the production of arms of sufficient quality and quantity to supply a militia and standing army. In order to supplement the production at Springfield and Harpers Ferry Armories, contracts were issued for private shops and makers to produce arms—these included Eli Whitney (pictured here) in New Haven, Connecticut; Simeon North in Middletown, Connecticut; and Lemuel Pomeroy, in Pittsfield, Massachusetts; among many others. Inspectors from the armories would ensure the terms of the contracts, which included standards and tolerances for parts, were met. (Courtesy of the Library of Congress.)

Most of the early buildings at Springfield Armory were constructed out of wood, which, in addition to being difficult to maintain (see Washington's comments in 1789), were susceptible to fire. After a fire wiped out several buildings in 1801, future construction began in brick and red sandstone quarried locally in Longmeadow, Massachusetts. The West Arsenal, pictured here in 1866, was intended to store finished muskets and other materials. Originally a two-story structure, it was completed about 1810, with a third floor added during the Civil War.

With the declaration of war against England in 1812, Springfield Armory struggled to meet the sudden demand for muskets. Supt. Benjamin Prescott, pictured, and his successor, Henry Lechler, were not only pressed to make new weapons, but also needed to repair older, broken weapons. Despite their best efforts and limited materials, only about 12,000 muskets were made per year during the war. Springfield Armory, along with Harpers Ferry, would have to find ways to improve their manufacturing capabilities to cope with sudden increases in demand when the country entered into large-scale conflicts.

Two

1815–1860

The War of 1812 was Springfield Armory's first test, and it was fairly successful. As an arms factory that was made largely from nothing less than 10 years before, there were still improvements to be made—both in its infrastructure and its processes. These dramatic changes marked the period beginning in 1815 through the eve of the Civil War.

Roswell Lee led the armory for 18 years as superintendent starting in 1815, overseeing dramatic improvements. Manufacturing sites were updated and modernized. The Water Shops, which were three separate sites along the Mill River, were upgraded with the goal of producing 30,000 muskets per year, double the previous annual production. The armory at the time employed about 400 workers total. To keep those employees focused on the ambitious production goals, Lee enforced strict rules. Shop hours were fixed to two five-hour shifts, more than two absences met with discipline, and rent was charged for armory housing. He also limited "scuffling or playing of Ball or other proceedings that have a tendency to impede . . . the progress of work." Correcting what was surely a problem, he declared, "From and after the 15th day of April 1816 no Rum, Gin, Brandy, Whiskey, or ardent Spirits of any kind will be suffered to be carried or drunk in or about the public work shops at this place."

By the time James Wolfe Ripley arrived in 1841, he was tasked with making similar improvements, but he clashed with the town (and in 1852, the city) of Springfield. He tore down many of the old buildings and constructed new ones, notably the commanding officer's quarters and the Main Arsenal. He also worked to increase and stabilize wages for the armorers, though he would not tolerate mistakes in manufacturing. In order to further his ideal manufacturing process, he dismissed large numbers of workers and brought in his own. The work that Ripley oversaw, though quite controversial at the time, left Springfield Armory with modern manufacturing facilities and processes that proved invaluable when the Civil War began.

Roswell Lee, a lieutenant colonel in the US Army, was officially appointed in July 1815 as a civilian superintendent of Springfield Armory. In the 18 years that Lee was in charge, the armory would make great progress and strides in production and quality of manufacture and achieve his personal goal of turning Springfield Armory into a "Grand National Establishment."

The green at the center of Armory Square at the Hill Shops, which still remains, took shape under Lee's administration. In the center of the green was a liberty pole, a symbol of the American Revolution borrowed from ancient Rome. In the workshops at the far end, the Model 1816 musket was assembled and finished. At a cost of about $10 per musket, Springfield Armory manufactured over 300,000 of these between 1816 and 1840.

Thomas Blanchard was a prolific inventor who was contracted by the armory in 1819 to produce musket stocks with machinery of his own invention. One of those machines was capable of reproducing irregular shapes, which had previously been done entirely by hand. The utilization of Blanchard's lathe was an important step toward the manufacture of interchangeable parts. His machine is still in the museum today.

Blanchard installed eight machines in the Lower Water Shops at the armory, which mechanized the process of "half-stocking" wood gunstocks, taking much of the laborious carving out of the process. While there were not any immediate improvements in cost savings, this was a dramatically important step toward the interchangeability of parts. Parts made on a machine were much more consistent than those made by hand. At first, Blanchard ran his own operation with his own workers and made between 32¢ and 37¢ per stock. Later, armory workers took over, and Blanchard was paid a 9¢ royalty per gunstock.

One of the largest operations on the hill, the massive Stocking Shop, caught fire on March 2, 1824. All of the sawdust and scraps, along with 15,000 black walnut stocks, quickly turned the building into an inferno. Armorers and citizens of Springfield turned out to help put out the fire. Their efforts were futile, and the blaze cost the armory about $20,000. The need to continue manufacturing prompted the construction of new, smaller shops on the site within a few months.

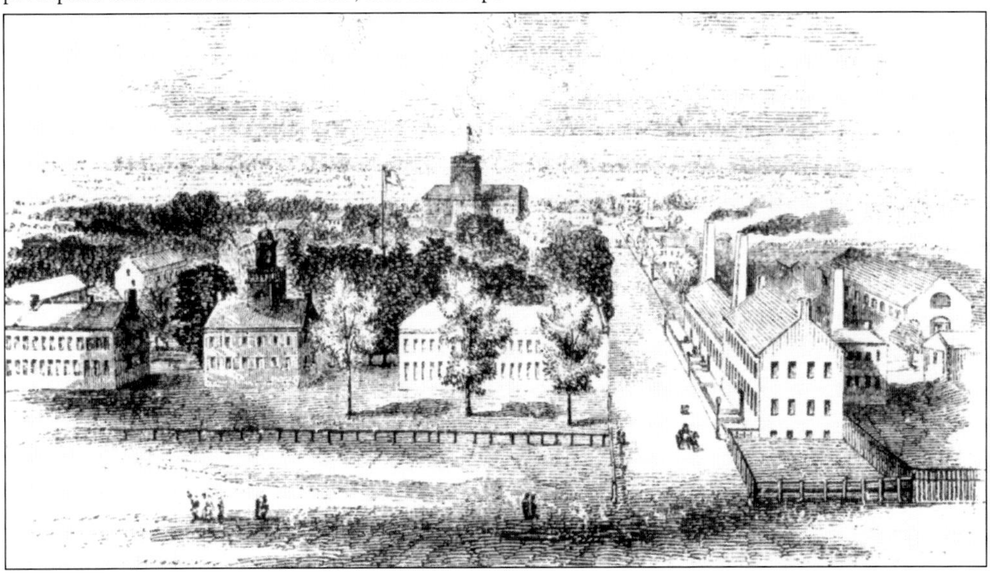

The three buildings in the left foreground were part of large construction projects in the 1820s. The administration building with a cupola is flanked by workshops that were constructed after the 1824 fire burned the large Stocking Shop. The second floor of the administration building was used as a nondenominational chapel. Episcopalians, Methodists, Baptists, Unitarians, and later Roman Catholics arrived in Springfield as armory workers before settling in the town.

As a teenager, Horace Smith, along with his brother and father, worked at Springfield Armory making bayonets as well as other musket parts. At the time, men were paid about 10¢ per bayonet. Smith would later leave the armory with this manufacturing knowledge and found Smith & Wesson, which still operates in Springfield.

Springfield Armory spent quite a bit of money on new machinery in the 1830s. Purchases included new waterwheels for grinding musket barrels, 22 forges in the Middle Water Shops, blast forges, and milling machines. Pictured here are the Upper Water Shops about 1830. The tall structure to the left was a boardinghouse for workers.

After a brief stint as a civilian superintendent, Maj. James Wolfe Ripley became the first military commandant of Springfield Armory in 1842. He instituted an aggressive program of construction that transformed the armory from an organic collection of shops and houses into a uniform, structured, military post.

Shortly after Ripley's arrival, the Model 1842 musket was adopted, and production began in 1844. This was the first firearm produced at both Springfield and Harpers Ferry Armories where the parts were interchangeable. This was an enormous milestone in industrial history and a critical achievement in military logistics. In the illustration at right, a lock assembler can now make a lock from a pile of parts without the need to track unique pieces.

Initially, the Model 1842 cost about $18 to manufacture, despite sophisticated machinery, as seen in this contemporary illustration of the forging room at the Water Shops. With improvements in manufacturing and as the armory worked out the kinks in procedures, costs dropped to about $11 per musket by the Mexican War and dropped again to about $8 by 1852.

"This is the Arsenal. From floor to ceiling, / like a huge organ, rise its burnished arms." Poet Henry Wadsworth Longfellow made a trip to Springfield Armory on his honeymoon in the early 1840s. The racks of finished muskets inspired him to write the poem "The Arsenal at Springfield" as a metaphor for the horrors of war.

Like Roswell Lee before him, James Ripley instituted sweeping overhauls of manufacturing and facilities, though with a much firmer hand. Shortly after Ripley's arrival, he completely shut down operations to refurbish the buildings. Old buildings, including the 1783 powder magazine, were torn down. Worker housing was razed to make room for manufacturing facilities, and employees were forced to live in town.

The downside of waterpower was its susceptibility to inclement weather. Frozen millponds in winter or droughts in summer limited water flow, which restricted the power needed to operate machinery. The armory purchased its first steam engine in 1843, which ushered in an era of consistent manufacture largely independent of the season. It also enabled machine operations to be moved to the hill, away from the Water Shops. Pictured here is the old steam engine at the Hill Shops, which ran for most of the last half of the 19th century.

In 1845, construction began on the massive commanding officer's quarters. This was seen by Ripley's opponents as a gross misuse of government funds.

The Main Arsenal was constructed in 1850 as a storehouse. The building was capable of holding 300,000 finished muskets. While much of Ripley's tenure at Springfield Armory was marked with local conflict, when Springfield incorporated as a city in 1852, it put the Main Arsenal at the top of the city seal.

Due to quarrels with the town, Ripley ordered a fence constructed around Armory Square on the hill. The original fence, made of wood pickets, was a quick and inexpensive solution. The fence was torn down several times by angry townsfolk when the disagreements with Ripley were especially tense. Ripley ordered the construction of a substantial stone and cast-iron fence around the site, which began in 1847 but was not completed until about 1860. The red sandstone foundations and pillars came from quarries nearby, and surplus, obsolete cannons were melted down for the fencing.

Construction on the Long Storehouse also began during Ripley's tenure. Seen above the pond in this 1870 image, the building was over 400 feet in length. The structure was intended as a storage area for raw materials, particularly black walnut for gunstocks. A small stable was also located there for the horses that were used in and around the armory.

The Water Shops were consolidated from three units to one state-of-the-art facility in the 1850s. In 1854, a British government delegation met Colonel Ripley to examine manufacturing at Springfield Armory. Since the armory had achieved the manufacture of interchangeable musket parts, the British group was interested in incorporating the process and methods back in England. This method was known as the American System of Manufacture.

In 1854, political winds shifted, and Congress rescinded the act putting military officers in charge of armories, despite objections from Secretary of War Jefferson Davis. Civilian control returned to Springfield Armory under the leadership of James Whitney, who oversaw the production of the Model 1855 rifle. It was the first rifled shoulder arm produced in mass quantities at the armory. Rifling is a series of lands and grooves inside a gun barrel that impart ballistic spin on a projectile, increasing accuracy and range.

In 1860, Virginian John Floyd, secretary of war under President Buchanan, ordered Springfield Armory to open its workshops to representatives from Georgia. They toured through the shops and all information about the manufacture of firearms was provided to them. Shortly after, Secretary Floyd ordered the shipment of over 100,000 muskets from Northern arsenals to the South.

Three

1861–1902

With the attack on Fort Sumter, the United States was thrown into civil war. Springfield Armory was suddenly required to increase production drastically to meet the sudden, though not surprising, demand. With some expansion of facilities, around 800,000 rifle-muskets were manufactured during the war by several thousand employees. Still, this was not enough. Northern contractors made tens of thousands more muskets to supply Union troops.

The years after the Civil War marked a drastic reduction in manufacturing and a strong push towards experimentation and innovation. Erskine Allin, master armorer at Springfield Armory, developed a system to utilize surplus musket parts to create a breech-loading rifle, which saved the government money, not only in parts, but in royalties as well. Allin's design served the military's immediate needs, but developments outside the country prompted the adoption of a new, foreign design called the Krag-Jorgensen, which could employ smokeless powder, significantly increasing range and accuracy.

As the United States began to test the waters of being a world power by declaring war with Spain in 1898, the Krag was put to the test in the hands of US Army Regulars, who found the design lacking. Captured Spanish Mauser rifles, judged far superior to the Krag by soldiers in the field, made their way back to Springfield Armory for testing and evaluation, as did varying designs of a new battlefield weapon—the automatic machine gun.

In 1864, the Hill Shops at Springfield Armory churn out arms in the midst of the Civil War.

With the outbreak of the Civil War in 1861, James Ripley, now a brigadier general and acting chief of ordnance, assigned Capt. A.B. Dyer (shown here) as commanding officer of Springfield Armory. From this point, Springfield Armory would remain under the administration of the US Army until its closure in 1968.

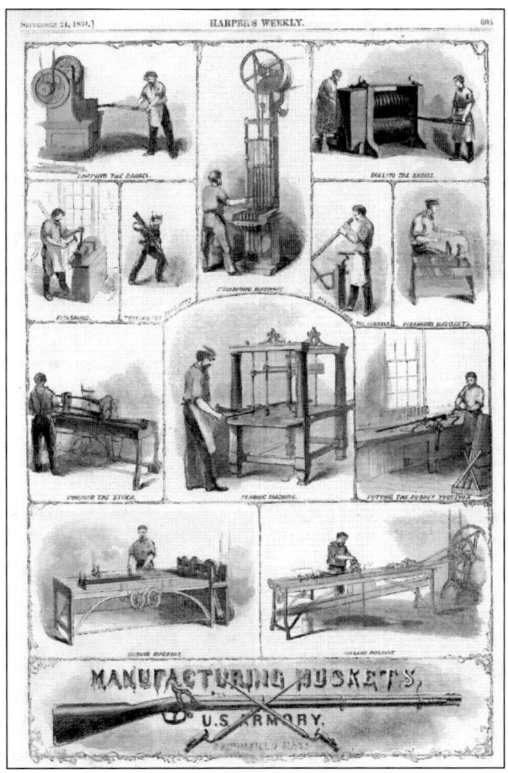

In order to meet the demands of war, the Model 1855 rifle-musket was trimmed down and designated the Model 1861. Parts deemed superfluous were eliminated, which also helped to speed up manufacture and save materials. This feature in the September 21, 1861, issue of *Harper's Weekly* illustrates several of the steps in manufacturing the rifle-musket.

Thomas Blanchard's original lathe came off the manufacturing line at Springfield Armory in 1855, after over 30 years in service. However, the initial design, where a pattern is duplicated on a wood blank, was in use during the Civil War (and well after), though with a much more compact design.

The long pieces of iron used for barrels were passed back and forth between workers on either side of the machine pictured here. The channels in the machine were successively smaller. As the red-hot iron was passed through each channel, the metal would lengthen and the outside diameter would shrink.

One of the last steps in making a barrel is rifling, which is measured in twists. Using the rifling machine above, a well-oiled cutter works its way along the bore inside the musket barrel. At a designated twist, the grooves of the rifling are cut a very small amount with each pass. The machine automated much of this process, ensuring precision and speeding up production.

Finally, all the individual pieces are put together. Because the process of interchangeable manufacture was well established at Springfield Armory by the Civil War, assemblers could put together rifle-muskets from piles of individual pieces. In contrast, the Confederacy had issues with consistency of weaponry and ammunition, which created a logistical issue the North did not have to contend with nearly as much.

The location of Harpers Ferry Armory in Virginia (later West Virginia) left it susceptible to attack. In 1861, it was burned to the ground by Union troops hoping to keep the machinery and weaponry out of Southern hands. Much of it was destroyed, but Confederates were still able to salvage machinery that was used to manufacture rifle-muskets in Richmond, Virginia, and Fayetteville, North Carolina. With the destruction of Harpers Ferry Armory, Springfield became the National Armory. (Courtesy of Harpers Ferry National Historical Park.)

In order to increase manufacturing space for the war effort, additions were built onto existing structures. The Middle Arsenal, seen here in a postcard from about 1900, was transformed from a storage building to manufacturing space. A steam engine was installed next to the building, which provided power to it and other structures around Armory Square.

Originally three separate buildings dating from the 1820s, these structures were combined into one large administration building during the war. The wings were used for manufacturing, while offices were concentrated in the center. From this vantage point at the intersection of State and Federal Streets, one can see the old Wait Monument in the foreground. (Courtesy of the Lyman and Merrie Wood Museum of Springfield History.)

The Machine and Polishing Shops were lengthened and updated, again to increase production capacity. This 1870s photograph captures the building at its full size. This structure would serve as the primary manufacturing site at the Hill Shops until new buildings were constructed in the 1890s.

The Water Shops were also upgraded during the war. Workers at the armory labored 10.5-hour days, six days a week; to keep up production, a night shift was added. This proved difficult as the new gas lighting installed at the shops was not very bright.

Because of its status as a government facility, Springfield Armory was self-insured against fire. They maintained a fire company through the 1800s and absorbed those costs as one of the expenses associated with manufacturing weapons. This 1866 photograph shows one of the fire companies, which could also be called to help fight fires in the city when needed.

Despite some rumors, there were no credible attacks against Springfield Armory during the Civil War. However, accidents did happen. Here, one of the workshops caught fire in the summer of 1864. Sabotage was ruled out, and the culprit was the buildup of emery dust in the sweltering attic of the polishing shop.

The firearm collection at Springfield Armory was started officially just after the Civil War, as a wide variety of weapons came back from the battlefields. Col. James G. Benton (right), commanding officer at the armory, recognized the need for a consolidated collection. He established the museum about 1866 and opened it to the public in 1871. In addition to being an attraction for tourists, the firearms were used by engineers and workers at the armory as a technical reference library. Below is an image of the museum about 1895. (Both, courtesy of the Lyman and Merrie Wood Museum of Springfield History.)

In this turn-of-the-20th-century postcard, the museum is clearly quite crowded. The museum was in several different locations at the armory over the years. It first started in the administration building and moved to a vacated section of the old Machine Shop before going to the Main Arsenal, where it remains today.

The junior officers' quarters were built in 1870. It is actually a duplex, with lower ranking officers and their families living in each half. This photograph was taken soon after the building was constructed.

The Main Arsenal was a popular tourist destination. Prior to World War I, attitudes about public property were different than they are today. As a taxpayer, one had the right to see how the money was spent—even during wartime. As long as the workers were not disturbed, visitors frequently came to the armory, especially to see the view off the top of the Main Arsenal's tower.

Taken from the top of the administration building looking west about 1875, this image shows the Main Arsenal across the green. To the left of the Main Arsenal is the paymaster's house, and to the right are the homes of the master armorer and the commanding officer. (Courtesy of the Lyman and Merrie Wood Museum of Springfield History.)

Pictured here is the view of the city of Springfield from the top of the Main Arsenal tower about 1885. This embodies the commanding presence the armory, and the Main Arsenal, had overlooking Springfield. Until larger buildings were constructed downtown in the 20th century, the Main Arsenal was the primary feature of the city's skyline.

Under the administration of Colonel Benton, Springfield Armory entered into a new era of scientific experimentation that persisted well after his death in 1881. Springfield Armory would become an important center of research and development in the 20th century. In this image, armory workers stand above the dam behind the Water Shops. The Water Shops pond, created by the dam, served as an early testing ground. Experimenting with different weapons and ammunition, engineers could fire from the Water Shops out to targets on the pond—up to ranges of 2,000 yards.

Those doing business with the armory in the 1850s and 1860s would enter Armory Square through the main gate on State Street (right). In the 1870s, the city lowered the street to install trolley tracks, and a new entrance was made at the corner of State and Byers Streets (below). Around World War I, a larger gate was made on Federal Street to accommodate a new technology—automobiles and trucks. The Byers Street gate became ceremonial, and the entrance on Federal Street became the third, and final, main gate.

Erskine Allin, master armorer of the Springfield Armory since 1848, worked to develop his own design for a breech-loading rifle, which became known as the "Trapdoor." His ingenious design reused parts already available from older muskets and appealed to the Army for its cost-effectiveness. Below is Allin's residence on the armory grounds as it appeared in 1866. The Trapdoor rifle and carbine were adopted after the Civil War, giving US troops a solid, breech-loading, single-shot weapon. It was used throughout the last half of the 19th century with about 650,000 of several models produced by Springfield Armory.

These group portraits were taken at the armory on September 30, 1886. Above is the Stocking Department, and below is the Milling Department.

Above is the Wood Department. Below are the workers of the Water Shops.

Beginning with the Centennial Exposition in Philadelphia in 1876, the armory had displays of artifacts from its museum as well as manufacturing displays at most of the large expositions, which occurred throughout the country in the decades after the Civil War. Above and below are images of Springfield Armory's manufacturing display in the Government Building at the 1893 World's Columbian Exposition in Chicago. The armory shipped out much of its manufacturing equipment and would actually make parts of the Trapdoor rifle for the exhibit. The display won several awards and recognitions for excellence.

In the late 1880s, there was a revolution in arms technology—the development of synthetic, smokeless propellant. This technology prompted major world powers to adopt new rifle designs that used this new ammunition to increase velocity and range over older, now obsolete, designs. The armory began construction on three new buildings in the vacant space at the Hill Shops known as Federal Square. These new buildings housed the Milling Department, the Machine and Filing Shops, and the Stocking Department. The modern facility began production on the newly adopted Krag-Jorgensen rifle.

The Krag-Jorgensen was a Norwegian design, adopted by the US Army in 1892. About 475,000 weapons of this design were manufactured through 1903. With the adoption of the Krag, the US military, and Springfield Armory, moved into the modern age. (Courtesy of the Lyman and Merrie Wood Museum of Springfield History.)

Four

1903–1935

With the turn of the 20th century, Springfield Armory was firmly in place as the National Armory of the United States. Not only did it oversee development and production of military shoulder arms, it was also responsible for the evaluation and testing of other small-caliber weapons, including pistols and machine guns.

Several features of the Mauser rifle, which impressed American soldiers during the Spanish-American War, were included in the new rifle developed at Springfield Armory, the Model 1903. While production on the new rifle began, testing and experimenting continued. Trials for a new sidearm were conducted at the armory, which resulted in the adoption of the Model 1911 pistol.

The United States stayed out of World War I until 1917, when Springfield Armory was caught unprepared. Despite a concerted effort to increase employment and production, the armory, even with help from other government manufacturing facilities such as Rock Island Arsenal, could not keep up with the sudden increase in demand. Alternative sources for rifles had to be sought out. Private manufacturers, which were already making rifles for the British, simply altered their designs for American ammunition and began producing what were called Model 1917 rifles to supplement armory production.

After the war, the armory continued research and development of an advanced semiautomatic rifle. Numerous designs were considered, but eventually the competition was reduced to two designs. One was developed independently by a prolific inventor named John Pedersen. The other was designed in-house by a civilian worker named John Cantius Garand, who was hired at Springfield Armory specifically for the semiautomatic rifle project. Garand's design was eventually chosen over Pedersen's, and the rifle, which Gen. George Patton called "the greatest battle implement ever devised," would soon be in the hands of the nation's soldiers in the biggest conflict the country had ever seen.

A sentry stands duty at the Byers Street gate about 1903.

Springfield Armory entered the 20th century with an expansion of manufacturing facilities. The Water Shops were extended in front of the dam, and a second matching tower was added onto the expansion. This dramatically increased manufacturing space for heavy machine work.

Pictured here are the Stocking Department (above) and the Milling Department (below) in September 1903. Unfinished Krag-Jorgensen stocks can be seen in the image above, though its time was over. The Spanish-American War and other conflicts had shown deficiencies in the Krag-Jorgensen design and its ammunition.

The Filing Shop (above) and the Machine Shop (below) are seen here as they appeared in September 1903. In replacement of the Krag, the US Army adopted the Model 1903 rifle a few months before these images were taken, and production of the new rifle began almost immediately. Over one million Model 1903s and variants were made at Springfield Armory.

In this calendar image from 1906, the cannon on the Hill Shops is fired in celebration of the Fourth of July. The armory made a lot of noise in celebration or remembrance. For example, to mark the death of Abraham Lincoln, 13 guns were fired at dawn, followed by a single shot every half-hour until dusk, when a volley from 36 guns rang out. (Courtesy of the Lyman and Merrie Wood Museum of Springfield History.)

Much of the machinery in use at the armory had been there for decades, and the equipment was modified, if necessary, to manufacture parts for new rifle designs. Note similarities between these images and those of Civil War manufacture. Above, a worker cuts inlets in stocks for the Model 1903 around 1905. Below, two men are rolling rifle barrels at the Water Shops around 1920. (Above, courtesy of the Lyman and Merrie Wood Museum of Springfield History.)

While many manufacturing processes were mechanized, one process remained firmly in human hands—straightening barrels. Nothing could give the accuracy of the human eye. Above is the "ring" method of barrel straightening and at right is the "line" method.

There were a number of groups that met outside of the regular workday for sports and other activities. There were basketball, tennis, and ice hockey teams at the armory through the 1960s. Pictured here is the Springfield Armory baseball team in 1906.

The armory's rifle team poses with their weapon of choice in 1924, the year they were the Industrial League Champions. One might say that the armory's team had a distinct advantage over other shooting teams from businesses and industries in the Springfield area.

In the Stocking Department, a structure built in Federal Square in the 1890s, workers add fittings to finished Model 1903 stocks.

At various stages in the barrel-making process, the barrels are inspected for quality. Here, a worker takes a look at an unfinished barrel that has yet to be bored out and rifled, among several other operations. (Courtesy of the Lyman and Merrie Wood Museum of Springfield History.)

In this 1920s image, workers inspect a variety of dimensions of unfinished receivers. Note the Army ordnance officer speaking with a man in the background. US Army officers oversaw many of the large departments at Springfield Armory, but most workers were civilians.

Once the individual parts are completed, they move to the assembly area, seen here in 1928, where finished pieces come together to make a complete Model 1903 rifle.

Because the United States did not enter World War I until 1917, after the war was raging for three years, Springfield Armory was caught off guard. Funding was not available until Congress declared war, and the armory scrambled to hire and train labor, purchase new machinery, and upgrade infrastructure in order to provide Model 1903 rifles to the Army. Despite their efforts, Springfield Armory would not be able to make enough rifles to meet the demand.

Pep rallies at the Water Shops, pictured above, and musical entertainment occurred regularly to keep employees motivated and engaged during the First World War.

At this flag-raising ceremony in August 1918, employees at the Water Shops gather with a contingent of soldiers. In order to increase security during the war, hundreds of soldiers were brought in. Barracks and other structures were built on the Hill Shops and the Water Shops to house them and ensure around-the-clock protection.

World War I marked the first time that women were employed in manufacturing at the armory. Here, women inspect parts to ensure they are within tolerance. (Courtesy of the Lyman and Merrie Wood Museum of Springfield History.)

Workers at the Hill Shops gather for a group photograph. In November 1918, there were 4,633 men and 748 women employed at Springfield Armory. Not only was this a dramatic increase in employees, but also a significant rise in diversity of gender and race in the workshops to levels never seen before.

World War I saw significant increase in the variety and lethality of military technology. In 1918, the Machine Gun School was started at Springfield Armory to familiarize and train Army officers and enlisted men in the various automatic weapons in use at the time. Above are the officers of the school, with Maj. Julian Hatcher, commanding, sitting front and center. Below, the officers practice fieldstripping a Hotchkiss—blindfolded.

The Machine Gun School included firing at Bircham Bend, an outdoor range a few miles from the armory. In the photograph above, officers try out a Vickers. Below is a class portrait in 1918. Note the different weapons spread out before the class.

Men and women of the armory line up for the Armistice Day parade in Springfield celebrating the end of the war. With the emergency over, operations at the armory dramatically declined. The daily production of 1,500 firearms in November 1918 was reduced to 1,000 in December and to 300 in February 1919.

While staffing and production were significantly reduced, experimentation and weapon development continued on a variety of projects. A new experimental building was constructed in 1919. Here, in one project, women load machine gun belts with ammunition (above), which were used to test and evaluate various machine gun designs (below).

To ensure the quality of the weapons still being produced and repaired, one rifle out of every day's production was fired to ensure functionality and accuracy (above), and one rifle out of each month's production was given a 12,000-round endurance test. Even the ammunition itself was tested with special Mann accuracy barrels (below). These and other tests at the armory expended nearly four million rounds of ammunition per year.

One of the most important projects at Springfield Armory was the development of a semiautomatic rifle. The Model 1903 was a bolt-action and had to be manually operated to fire each round. A light rifle that could automatically cycle the empty cartridge and load a new one with each pull of the trigger had enormous military potential. In 1919, John C. Garand was hired to specifically work on this project. Above is Garand's work area, known as the Model Shop, in the midst of his efforts in 1924.

The wife and daughter of Colonel Schull, commanding officer of Springfield Armory from 1924 to 1929, sit by a decorative pool on Armory Square. This area of the Hill Shops was meticulously maintained, as it served as a social center for the military families living there, along with visiting guests and dignitaries.

In the old days, parts and supplies would move between the different armory sites by horse and wagon. Later, an electric train and large trucks did the job.

In 1931, disaster struck the armory's museum. Oily rags, used to clean the collection, were piled by a radiator. In the middle of a cold night, the heat turned on and the pile of fabric spontaneously combusted, starting a fire that damaged many historical weapons. The museum collection was cleaned up as best as possible, but the damage was done. Above is the museum as it appeared before the fire, and below is the museum after cleanup.

The main administration building on the Hill Shops is pictured about 1928. With costs dramatically cut after World War I, the number of officers and employees with Springfield Armory was the smallest in decades. However, stirrings in Europe and Asia would change all that, and the armory would not be caught unprepared again.

Five

1936–1945

All of the previous decade's work developing a semiautomatic weapon was about to pay off. Shortly after the Army adopted John Garand's design in 1936, Springfield Armory went through a series of upgrades to infrastructure, primarily through the employment of Works Progress Administration (WPA) crews.

But the biggest boost came after Adolf Hitler ordered the invasion of Poland in September 1939, along with much of Europe in the following months. With great foresight, the armory's budget was increased by 250 percent. Massive construction and planning commenced. When the United States declared war in 1941, Springfield Armory, in stark contrast to earlier wars, was prepared to produce the semiautomatic M1 rifle by the millions, quickly putting the most advanced battle rifle into the hands of soldiers.

In order to accomplish this, employment skyrocketed and became much more diverse. Women made up 43 percent of the workforce, numbering about 13,500 at its peak. Shifts working 24 hours a day produced 3.5 million M1 rifles. At the peak of production, the rate was 164 M1 rifles per hour, which stands in stark contrast to the initial production of the old Charleville pattern, Model 1795, at 245 muskets that entire year. Springfield Armory had come a long way in a century and a half.

Production at the armory was also simplified; only M1s and a few other items needed for the war effort were manufactured. This resulted in a surprising reduction in workforce starting in 1943, even before the war was close to resolution. As the supply of M1s coming from Springfield Armory met the demand, thousands of employees were slowly let go before a significant drop just after the surrender of Japan.

In 1936, the US Army officially adopted the M1 rifle. Also known as the "Garand" after its inventor, the M1 would go into production that year. Not only did John Garand (above) develop the weapon design at Springfield Armory, he also invented the machinery and processes by which it would be manufactured. Garand continued this work as the armory began to upgrade.

As part of Pres. Franklin Delano Roosevelt's New Deal, the WPA sent work crews to the armory to upgrade facilities and infrastructure. A new 200-yard underground firing range was attached to the Experimental Building. It was kept underground to reduce noise heard by residents on nearby Pearl Street.

Most armory buildings were painted after their initial construction. All buildings were sandblasted down to bare brick by the WPA, including the commanding officer's quarters (above).

Roads also received an overhaul by the WPA work crews. Until this point, many of the interior thoroughfares were dirt. The armory received new concrete roadways, which doubtless provided a much more reliable surface for materials moving between buildings.

Like the displays at the expositions in the 1800s, Springfield Armory, along with other area businesses and industries, exhibited at the Eastern States Exposition in West Springfield every year. This is the exhibit in 1936. The "Big E" still holds one of the largest fairs in the country each fall, as it has since 1914.

In September 1938, an enormous hurricane blew down on New England. Not many areas escaped unscathed. This view from the top of the Main Arsenal shows damage to trees and roadways in Armory Square. Some buildings were also damaged, but production was not drastically affected.

The first M1 off the production line was completed in August 1937, and production started at about 200 rifles per day. These are images from early 1940, when production had been going on for several years. At left, a worker operates the drop forge in the Water Shops. Below, thousands of barrels are in process.

Handwork persisted in several facets of manufacturing, particularly early in the history of the M1 rifle, as the photograph at right from September 1940 reveals. Below, finished rifles are assembled before being sent to the packing department.

Production could only go so far without modern facilities. The tipping point came from Europe, when Nazi Germany invaded numerous countries. With the fall of France in May 1940 came a dramatic increase in funding for Springfield Armory. A few months later, Springfield Armory began construction on a massive, state-of-the-art manufacturing facility known as Building 104.

Upon completion of the main parts of the building, machinery was quickly moved from the old shops. Milling machines, lathes, and grinders, among many other items, were moved and then put right back into operation with very little production time lost. When Building 104 was completed, the production rate for the M1 rifle increased five times over.

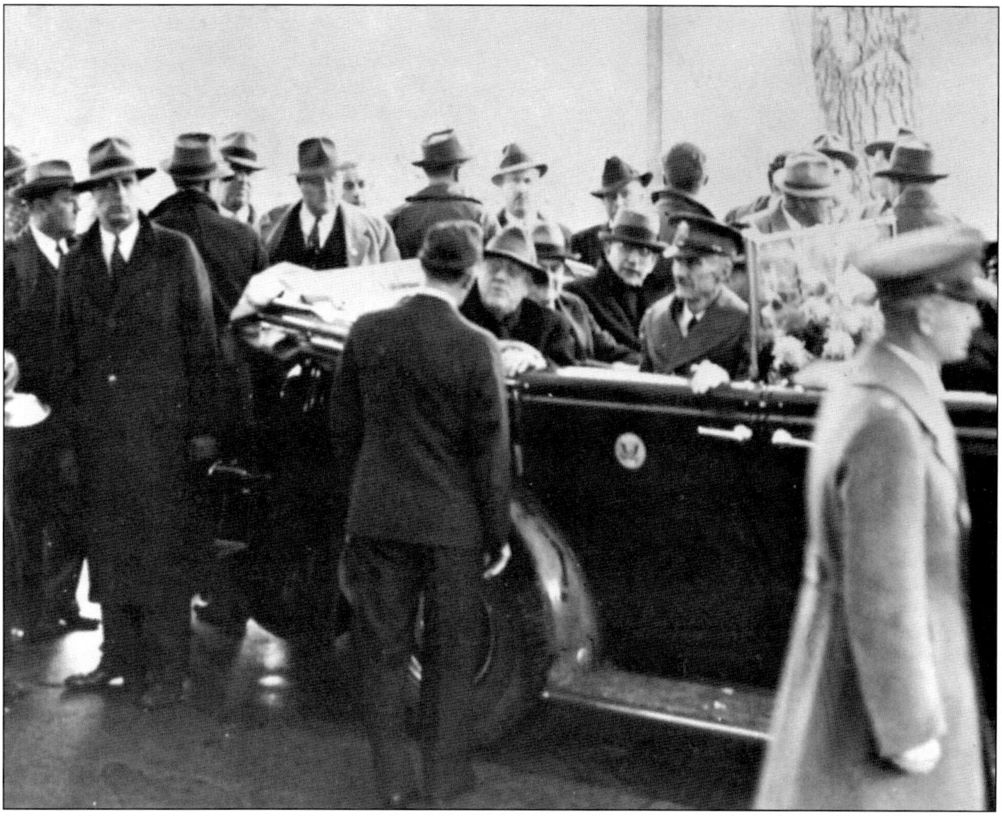

In October 1940, President Roosevelt visited Springfield Armory while campaigning for the upcoming elections. In addition to making a speech next to the new manufacturing building, he also took some time to talk with John Garand. Garand is seen above with his back to the camera as he speaks to the president.

On December 7, 1941, Japan attacked Pearl Harbor, and the United States was soon at war. However, Springfield Armory would not be caught scrambling to suddenly increase production as with previous conflicts. By this time, the armory was already making 1,100 M1 rifles every eight hours, with workers producing around the clock in three shifts.

The third shift ran from 11:00 p.m. to 7:00 a.m. Building 104 was completely lit by fluorescent fixtures, the first in the nation with that much artificial light. This enabled work to progress throughout the night. Above is an image of the interior of Building 104, featuring the Milling Department working in the evening.

In 1941, the armory greeted two special guests, Charles Burt and George Stebbins, who had both worked at Springfield Armory as teenagers during the Civil War. The 93-year-old men were shown the new facilities in Building 104, where this image was taken. One holds a brand-new M1 rifle, while the other holds a Model 1863 rifle-musket.

New employees flowed into Springfield Armory. After hiring, employees had their photographs taken (above) and went to the infirmary for a battery of tests to ensure their fitness for work. Dr. Helen Richards headed the infirmary, which was in the former master armorer's quarters.

Women came to work in large numbers—nearly 6,000 women, called Women Ordnance Workers (or WOWs), were employed at Springfield Armory. WOWs were given special bandanas, which not only identified them as ordnance workers, but also provided protection by keeping hair away from running machinery. At left, Rita Murphy models the new bandana, while two employees (below) sort bandanas before giving them out.

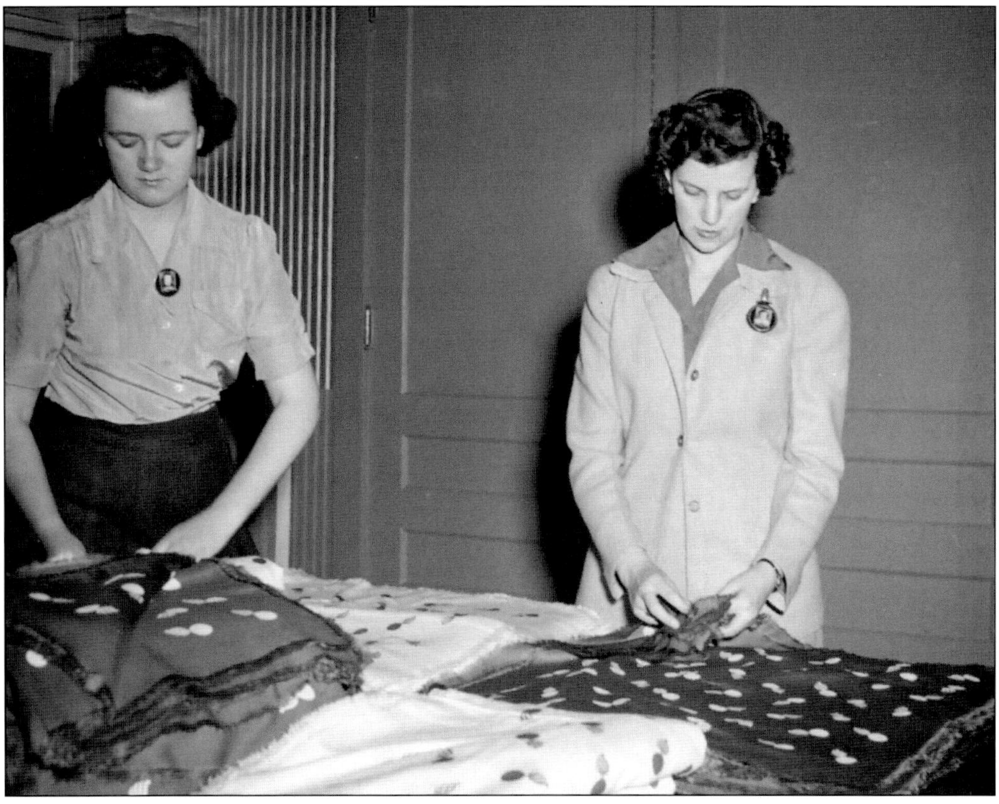

Young people came to work at the armory during the war as well. Priscilla Bryant, a local high school student, worked a shift after school sorting and inspecting en-bloc clips for the M1 rifle. Another worker in a similar situation noted that she made more money than her father by working second shift at the armory after school.

The workers were also provided with a number of benefits, including athletic activities and child care. In the image above, from left to right, Harriet McDonald, Mrs. Charles Warner (instructor), Betty Brissette, Florence Bernardi, and Bertha Robinson practice archery on Armory Square. A small child-care facility was set up across the street from the Hill Shops at the High School of Commerce on State Street (below).

In an effort to train new employees who may have little-to-no experience in manufacturing, an apprentice school was established, which would find success training skilled and unskilled workers through the 1960s. Above, a woman learns how to use a milling machine, and another apprentice learns the technique of brazing (below).

After any necessary training, employees got right to work. Helen Cathcart operates an automatic shaper (above), and Jennie Jedzniak assembles M1 receivers (left).

The days of belt-driven machinery are gone, though the machines themselves stayed. With new electric motors on each machine, the Rifling Department works on M1 barrels.

Finished M1 rifles are packed up and shipped out by the thousands every day. Pictured here, the Packing Department places the rifles in special bags and crates that provide protection during shipment.

In September 1942, Springfield Armory received the prestigious Army-Navy "E" Award for excellence in production. A break in manufacturing was called so that all employees could be at the ceremony. Commanding officer Colonel McFarland addressed the crowd, and a detachment of Native American soldiers served as honor guard.

Springfield Armory as a whole received the award, but outstanding individuals were also recognized. Wilbur Ancrum, foreman of the Heat Treat Shop, receives his "E" pin from Maj. Gen. Sherman Miles.

Charles Hills (above) grinds barrels while an unidentified worker runs a broaching machine (right), cutting the interior faces of receivers. During the war, African Americans made up about 5 percent of the male workforce at Springfield Armory and about 11 percent of female employees.

Mary Smith became the first woman to operate a drop forge machine. Work on the jarring forges had been a job traditionally held by men, but at the peak of employment, there were not many duties that women did not perform.

In 1943, the Springfield Armory hired 10 blind employees. After training in the apprentice school, two men and two women served as inspectors, ensuring tight tolerance on individual parts. The men in the photograph above are inspecting firing pins.

While many jobs involved direct work on the manufacturing line, there were other supporting positions that were just as important. Tools and cutters had to be regularly inspected to ensure they would function properly. Here, a gentleman inspects a rifling broach, used as part of the process to cut rifling in the barrels.

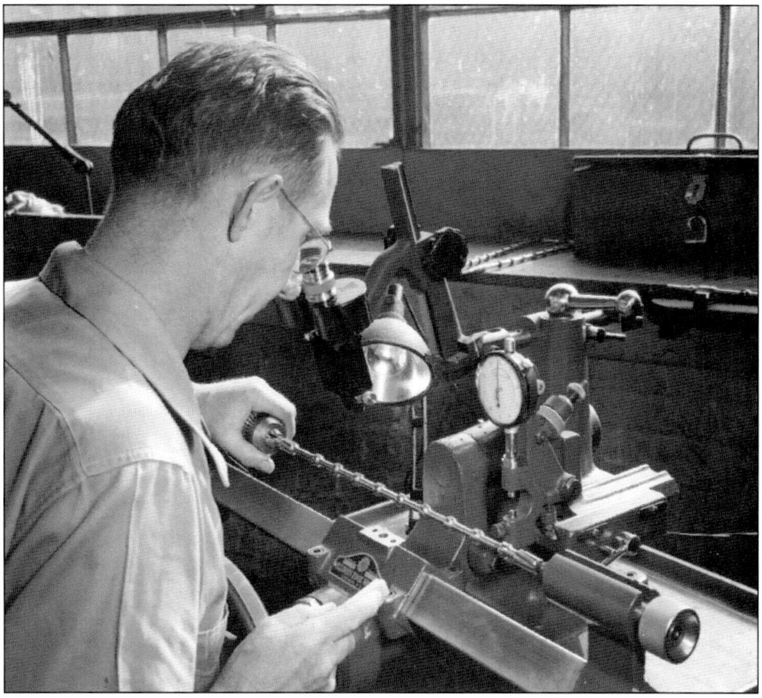

The chemical lab in Building 104 had numerous duties, which included testing incoming raw materials for quality and experimentation with different chemical treatments for parts.

In September 1943, the armory's workers were in for a special treat. As part of a large tour to war plants around the country, Benny Goodman played an employee-only concert on armory grounds. Only employees and their guests were admitted to the concert, but the music was broadcast over the radio until 10:00 p.m.

After 10:00 p.m., Benny Goodman and his band continued in a private performance. Below, Goodman and drummer Gene Krupa take a bow at the end of the show.

Organizing thousands of paychecks is difficult work, particularly on payday. Above, Frank Sheehan and John Garvey sort paychecks before they are distributed to the shops. Once at the individual shops (below), the workers line up to get their checks.

Despite the heavy work schedule, there was still time for fun and a bit of silliness. Above, a woman poses with two armory guards who look quite creepy in their First World War gas masks and helmets. Below, Marguerite Jenks was doubtless the center of attention in her office when the baby skunk made an appearance.

In an effort to keep up morale, a monthly newsletter was produced for all employees. The newsletter featured stories from the armory, news about employees (there were many instances of workers meeting and marrying during the war), jokes, and other features.

Legend has it that John Garand loved ice-skating so much that he flooded parts of his house, opening windows during winter to make an indoor rink. The armory's photography lab created this image to illustrate the story for publication in the *Armory News*.

John Garand, as a chief engineer and head of the Model Shop, was elevated to legendary status after his M1 design proved so successful. Garand continued to work on many projects during the war, including one to turn the semiautomatic M1 into a fully automatic rifle, in preparation for the possible invasion of Japan.

After the peak level of almost 14,000 employees at the armory in 1943, the workforce was slowly downsized. Some soldiers who worked at the armory before the war returned to their jobs, and thousands of others were let go. Before V-J Day, there were over 3,000 employees in the Manufacturing Division alone. Only two weeks after Japan's surrender, that number was drastically reduced to about 900. The war was over.

Six

1946–1968

With a significant reduction in employment, production of the M1 rifle stopped. A marked shift in policy moved primary responsibility for manufacturing shoulder arms away from Springfield Armory and into the hands of contractors. The primary role for the armory moving forward would focus on the research and development of new weapon systems.

Foremost in research projects was the development of a lightweight, select-fire, infantry rifle. The semiautomatic M1 served the military well through the last war, though it was clear that a full-automatic rifle, light enough for individual use, was preferred. Numerous designs were tested, until the M14, a close relative of the M1, was adopted in 1957. In addition to the M14, Springfield Armory also developed a number of other successful systems during these years, including the M60 machine gun, the M79 grenade launcher, and the M61 Vulcan aircraft gun.

Research and development at Springfield Armory was nothing new. This kind of experimentation had been going on for nearly a century. From the development of the Trapdoor rifle, the Model 1903, and, perhaps most significantly, the Garand M1 rifle, Springfield Armory proved again and again that it was up to the task of providing shoulder arms for the US military. Still, this was not enough to justify its continued existence, and, as part of cost-cutting measures by the Department of Defense, Springfield Armory began to phase out in 1964.

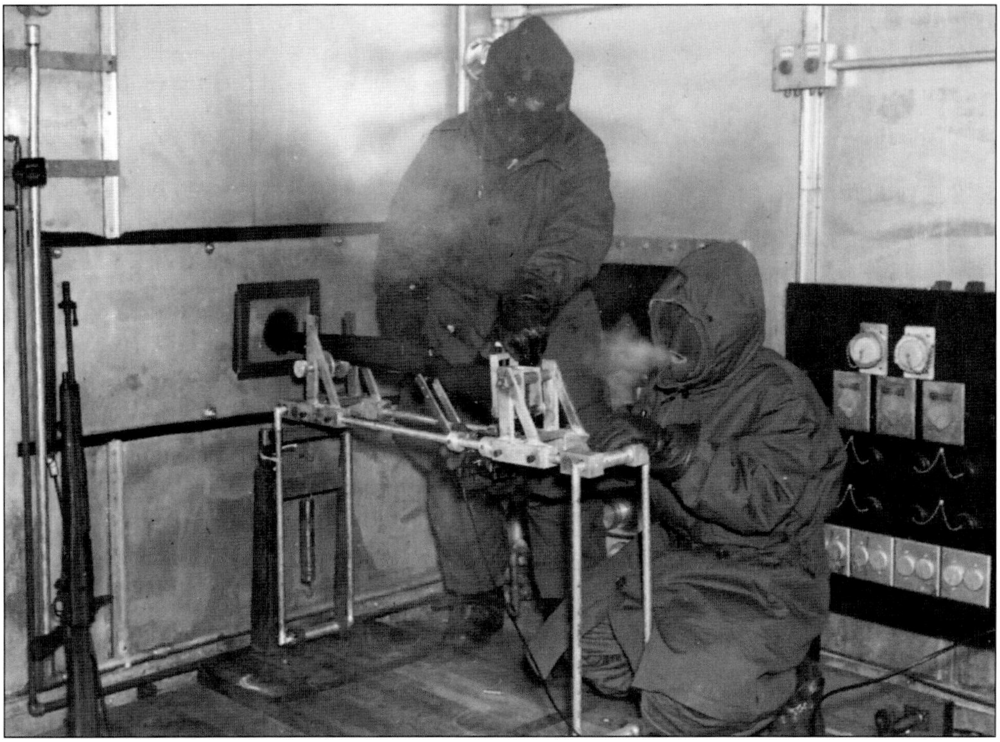

Springfield Armory shifted to a testing and development role as it worked to find a lightweight select-fire rifle and other weapons for the military. One of the ways these designs were tested was in a special climatic room, which could reach temperatures of negative 65 degrees Fahrenheit. These experiments were important both for testing use in arctic climates and the functionality of aircraft weapons in higher atmosphere temperatures.

Production of the M1 rifle resumed with the outbreak of the Korean War, and the armory produced about 640,000 M1s through the late 1950s. Above is the latest iteration of the Blanchard lathe, utilizing an oversize pattern to ensure detailed contours. The receiver broaching line is shown below.

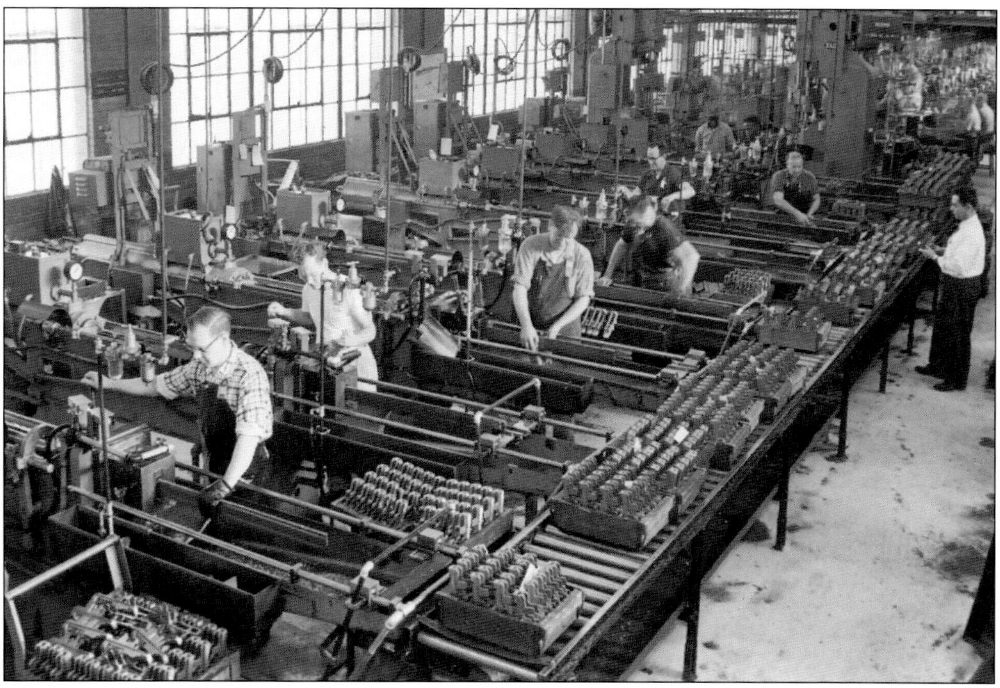

The armory also produced heavy machine guns in the postwar period. M3 machine guns are assembled in the image above, while side plates for the M85 tank machine gun are forged at the Water Shops (below).

In 1957, the Army adopted two new weapon systems, both developed at the Springfield Armory. The M14 rifle was a descendant of the M1 rifle, though it had the capability to select between semiautomatic and full automatic, among many other differences. The M60 was a belt-fed light machine gun developed out of research into German automatic weapons used in World War II. Springfield Armory sent a team out to demonstrate these new weapons to soldiers at Fort Devens in 1959. Above, soldiers examine the new weapons while an armory employee demonstrates the M60 below.

Demonstrations were also given to the public, as awareness and support of the armory and its mission was critical. Here, four employees give a demonstration of the armory's latest products in front of crowds at the Eastern States Exposition in West Springfield.

The M14 shared several components with the M1 rifle, and most of the same machinery could be used. Once the production line was up and moving, Springfield Armory manufactured about 160,000 M14s over the next decade. Among several other new advances in production, the armory started using precision casting to make smaller parts. Molds are made in the image above, and once ready, molten metal is poured into the form (below).

One thing that remained constant throughout the armory's production from the very first Charleville-patterned musket to the M14 was black walnut stocks. Pictured here is the Stocking Department in 1962.

Over the years, Springfield Armory went through tons of wood, and local schools could expect plenty of scrap walnut for woodshop projects. This machine is an automatic router. Rotating cutter heads following cam paths produce the barrel channel and other internal cuts as the table rotates around.

More and more sophisticated equipment was available for analysis and testing on experimental weapons, in-process weapons, and even spot checks on finished firearms. Employee Rocco Calabrese inspects a cracked part using magnetic particles. The particles collect in any fissure or crack and enable the defects to be more easily located.

A borescope is used to inspect the interior face of the M14 barrel (above). Later, completed parts go through final inspection. Springfield Armory was a leader in the concepts of quality assurance during production and quality control once production was complete.

Finished M14s are assembled above. The rifles are then tested on several points, including function and endurance. At right, an M14 goes through a function-firing test on full automatic.

Most weapons were produced by contract after World War II. By Army policy, internal manufacturing sites would be limited to pilot production runs. The M14 was made by Winchester, TRW, and Harrington & Richardson, in addition to Springfield Armory. In order to ensure weapons made by different manufacturers were interchangeable, tests were conducted at Springfield Armory with the contractors present. Random rifles from each source were pulled apart, mixed up, and reassembled.

Here, M79 grenade launchers, also developed at Springfield Armory, go through an interplant interchangeability test. Representatives from the contractor, Knarr Corporation, watch as their M79s and those from Springfield Armory are disassembled, mixed, and reassembled. These tests occurred monthly with all contracts.

As Springfield Armory took on more research and development projects, new test facilities were needed. Building 300 (above) was constructed as a machine-gun testing facility and was located at the railhead off Page Boulevard, which historically was the place raw materials came by rail to the armory. For projects requiring a large amount of space, a facility was set up on Quabbin Reservoir (below). At this site, large weapons could be tested, such as antiaircraft weaponry, which needed to fire up in the air or in other directions that could not be done indoors.

The 20-millimeter Vulcan, designated the M61, was a partnership development between Springfield Armory and General Electric and one of the armory's most successful projects in its later years. The M61 was a multi-barreled weapon that operated much like the old Gatling guns of the late 1800s and was intended for Air Force fighter jets and other applications. The Vulcan had a rate of fire of about 6,000 rounds per minute.

Because of the fast firing cycles of the Vulcan, the M14, M60, and other weapons, high-speed filming equipment was set up in the testing facilities. Once captured on film, the technicians and engineers could see actions work in slow motion and spot any issues that could not be inspected in real time.

On April 2, 1963, a formal dedication ceremony took place making Armory Square, the oldest part of Springfield Armory, a National Historic Landmark. Numerous guests took part in the dedication, including John Garand, who retired from the armory in 1953 and is shown below unveiling the commemorative plaque mounted on the administration building.

While limited production concentrated on the M14, operations also involved refurbishing and repairing old M1s and upgrading pistols and rifles for the National Matches, an annual shooting competition. At right, M1 rifle bores are scrubbed prior to disassembly, when the parts would be ultrasonically cleaned. In addition to making National Match rifles and pistols, the armory also sent out repair teams to the national competitions at Camp Perry, Ohio (Below, courtesy of the Lyman and Merrie Wood Museum of Springfield History.)

In 1964, the apprentice school marked its 25th anniversary. Numerous students were trained over the years. In the above photograph, a class is given on Advanced Electronically Controlled Machine Tools, an eight-week course that included pertinent mathematics, electronics, hydraulics, and programming. Below, instructors Norman Smith, Floyd Williams, Alan Stewart, and William Loftus examine a drawing.

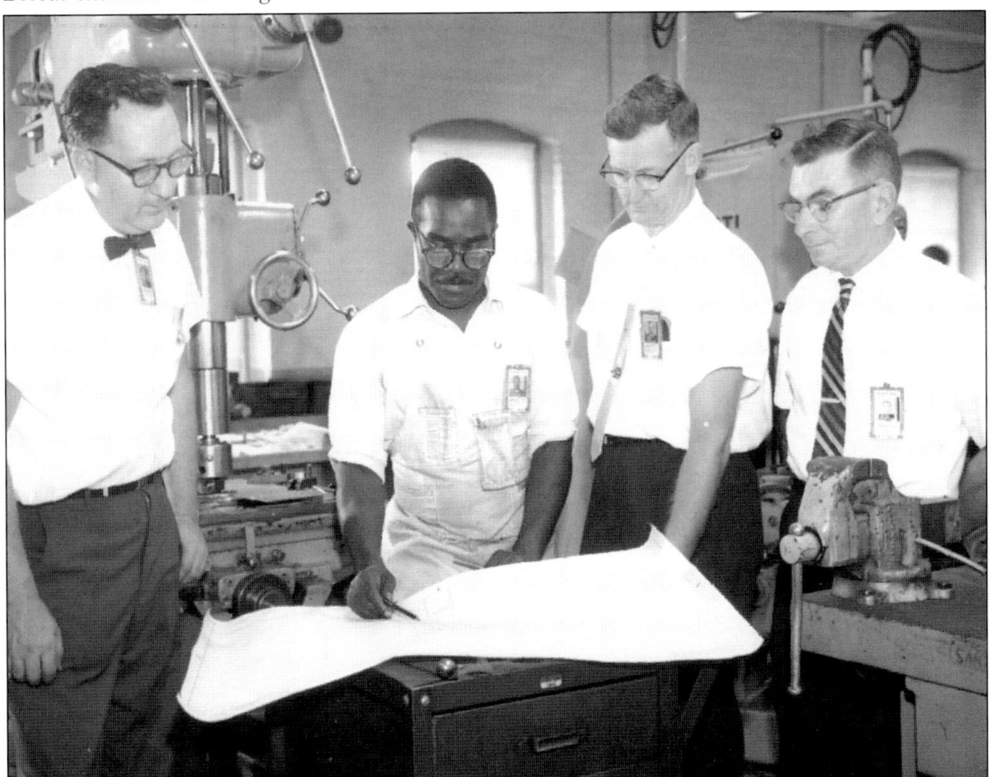

As the Army moved towards helicopters as an operational combat vehicle, Springfield Armory was tasked with developing several weapons systems. Armory engineers worked to integrate control systems in the cockpit with externally mounted weaponry. Earl Grant and John Hogan, electronics proof technicians, examine a helicopter weapons-aiming system and a minigun mounted alongside.

Variations of the M60 were also developed that could be mounted in an open door of the helicopter (left) or alone or in pairs on each side (below).

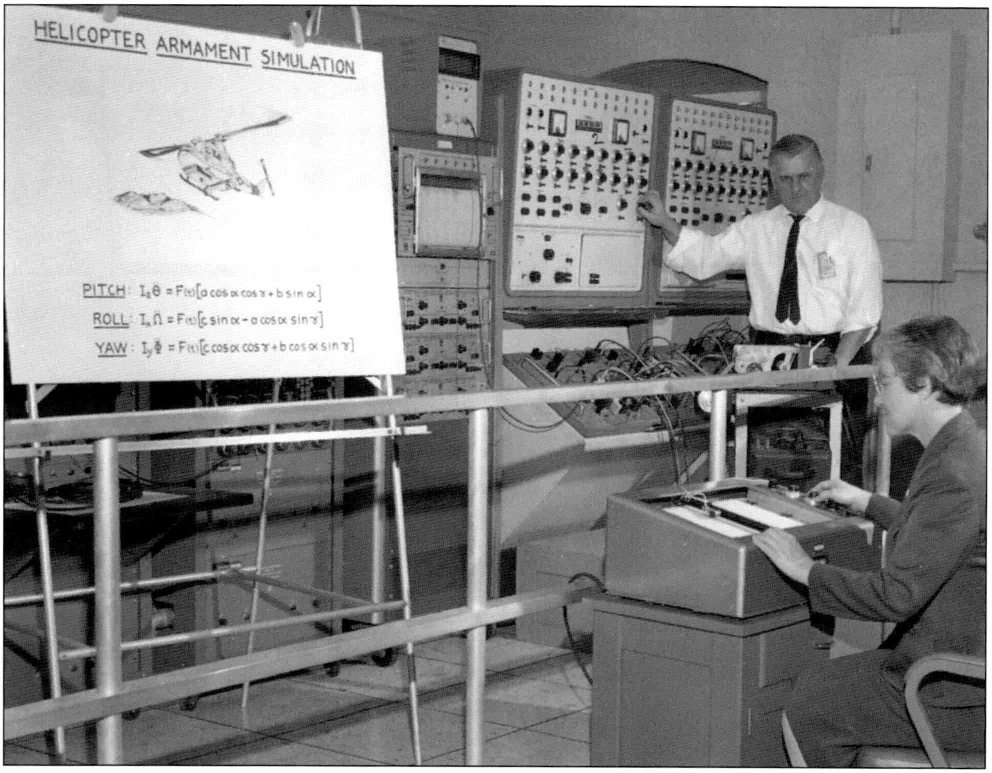

Sophisticated computers were used to run simulations of helicopter flight and to take into account any issues with the addition, or the firing, of different weaponry in various configurations. These could be tested in real time at the Quabbin Range (below).

In the 1960s, the arrival of the AR-15, and later the M16, demonstrated several things aside from its functionality. For one, the weapon was developed by a private company. This was nothing new, but in combination with the fact that private industry had shown its ability to mass-produce weapons to the satisfaction of the military was a death knell for Springfield Armory.

The decision to close Springfield Armory came on November 19, 1964. Secretary of Defense Robert McNamara determined that the armory was "excess to the needs of the federal government" and should be closed within four years.

A delegation from Massachusetts met Secretary McNamara at the Pentagon in February 1965 to present a counter-argument to the closure decision. The delegation consisted of senators Leverett Saltonstall and Edward Kennedy, representatives Edward Boland and Silvio Conte, Gov. John Volpe, Springfield mayor Charles Ryan, and numerous other local representatives.

McNamara visited Springfield Armory on March 17, 1965, to meet the delegation that had traveled to Washington the previous month. Here, he toured the armory and listened to further arguments for its retention. In the photographs above, McNamara speaks during a press conference at Springfield Armory while Senator Kennedy, Representatives Boland and Conte, Governor Volpe, Mayor Ryan, and others look on.

By November 1965, McNamara reviewed the case and announced that he would uphold his original decision to close the armory, citing savings as a major influence. Research and development functions would be moved to other US Army arsenals, and manufacturing would be bid out to private contractors. The local community was distraught at the loss of jobs and an institution that had been a part of Springfield since American independence.

As Springfield Armory slowly closed down, buildings were emptied, machinery sold at auction, and functions moved away. Employees were given retirement packages or offered employment at other, faraway facilities. Industries purchased some buildings, hoping to establish themselves in the city and retain some labor. The State of Massachusetts purchased a part of Armory Square, and Springfield Technical Institute, now Springfield Technical Community College, started moving into some of the most historical buildings. On April 30, 1968, employment was reduced to zero, and Springfield Armory closed its doors forever.

Bibliography

Bauer, Frank. *At the Crossroads: Springfield, Massachusetts, 1636–1975.* Springfield, MA: Bicentennial Committee of Springfield, 1975.

Chapin, Charles Wells. *Sketches of the Old Inhabitants and Other Citizens of Old Springfield.* Springfield, MA: Press of Springfield Printing and Binding Company, 1893.

Clark, David, ed. *Arms for the Nation: Springfield Long Arms.* Export, PA: Scott Duff Publications, 1994.

Deyrup, Felicia. *Arms Making in the Connecticut River Valley: A Regional Study of the Economic Development of the Small Arms Industry, 1798–1870.* York, PA: G. Shumway, 1970.

Dvarecka, C.L. *Springfield Armory: Pointless Sacrifice.* Ludlow, MA: Prolitho Publishing, 1968.

Ezell, Edward. "The Death of the Arsenal System: The Decision to Close Springfield Armory." Paper presented at the annual meeting of the Organization of American Historians, Dallas, TX, April 18, 1968.

Green, Constance McLaughlin. "History of Springfield Armory." Unpublished manuscript, last modified 1945.

Rayle, Roy E. *Random Shots: Episodes in the Life of a Weapons Developer.* Bennington, VT: Merriam Press, 2006.

Rosenberg, Nathan, ed. *The American System of Manufactures.* Edinburgh: University Press, 1969.

Whittlesey, Derwent. "Springfield Armory: A Study in Institutional Development." PhD diss., University of Chicago, 1920.

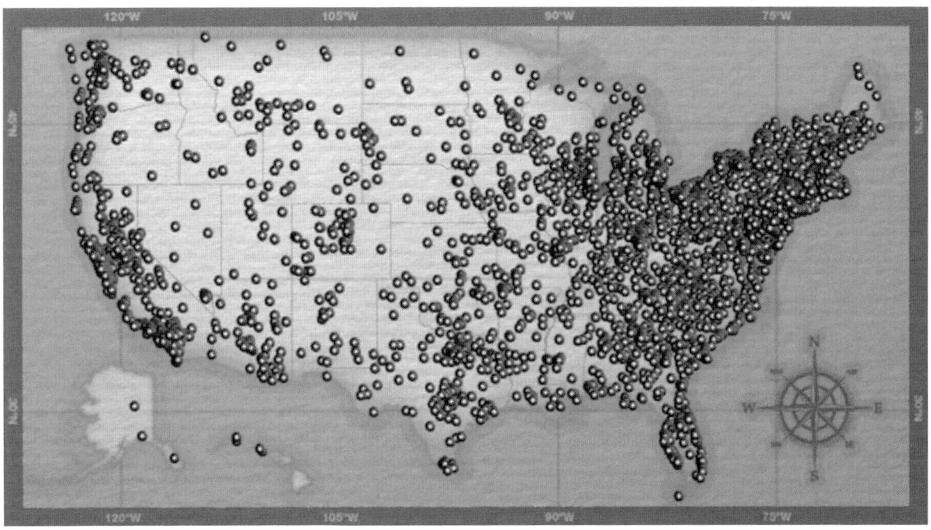